MOVING TO CLIMATE CHANGE HOURS

Other Titles by Ross Belot

Swimming in the Dark

MOVING TO CLIMATE CHANGE HOURS

ROSS BELOT

JAMES STREET NORTH BOOKS

James Street North Books is an imprint of Wolsak and Wynn Publishers.

Cover and interior design: Jared Shapiro
Cover image: Stock photo *Dirty City* retrieved from Envato Elements with
permission
Interior images: Ross Belot
Author photograph: Ross Belot
Typeset in Crimson Text
Printed by Coach House Printing Company Toronto, Canada

The publisher gratefully acknowledges the support of the Ontario Arts
Council, the Canada Council for the Arts and the Government of Canada.

James Street North Books
280 James Street North
Hamilton, ON
Canada L8R 2L3

Library and Archives Canada Cataloguing in Publication

Title: Moving to climate change hours / Ross Belot.
Names: Belot, Ross, author.
Description: Poems.
Identifiers: Canadiana 20200166115 | ISBN 9781989496121 (softcover)
Classification: LCC PS8603.E485 M68 2020 | DDC C811/.6—dc23

For Sara

TABLE OF CONTENTS

I

FIRST DAY

Gulf Oil refinery Clarkson, Ontario, 1979

Two men blinded by hydrofluoric acid
yesterday. The skin of one
absorbed acid
               and it ate his bones.
He died this morning.
The gate's safety sign says
12 hours worked
since the last lost time.

The safety trainer lectures.
Hydrogen sulphide.
At high concentrations it causes olfactory paralysis,
you can't smell it. Then you fall down
unconscious and next you die. If you see a body
on the ground
you must:
               check wind direction,
               move upwind,
               call for help.
Imagine your best friend Bill
on the ground,
how it would feel to leave him.

This is your first day,
wear workboots, learn work rules,
get the paycheque, go home to Shelley
pregnant with Neil, looking after little Heather –
do the right thing, be a good boy,
come home safe
ten thousand more times.

HIGHWAY 6

Sure I see Erv, dressed in blue coveralls, rusted oil
refinery boiling behind, warm grip of his hand on my shoulder.

Sure, I drove to work thousands of times
over years, that same route,
the one where I almost died, a slide
on April snow, head-on
into two cars. Not far from
where Erv drove his SUV directly

into a transport truck. Erv's body landed in its cab through the
windshield, the driver wrecked for life. Erv's supporters
at work said he must have been tired, Erv's trial for Erv's
wife's murder wearing him down.

The truck driver said Erv looked right at him as he drove into the
transport's front grill.

RAILWAY STORY

i walked the tracks to   high school from high school

taking chances   bending

rules   those tracks

led to trouble   in other ways

the cannabis cemetery   parties and ostensible

indifference working   in the railway yard summer

i changed   kicking up sulphur

on railbeds   crossing non-existent mills and fertilizer

plants steel   toed re-enforced

to protect feet   broken-down

pinto dusty   green ford fairlane

my belt line trips   watch a man's life sliding

liquor beside him   singing over his radio

lying on a flatcar   as they roll together

around the corner

subway trains to   new life's office

smaller and harder   a long way from walking

lines in late night nadir   yeasty odour

of Port Colborne   flour box

cars the new   oily steel's smell

Dofasco sunday still   that shriek

steel on steel tunnels   bored through earth

likened to dark   nights surrounded steel

both sides   walking lines

wrote it   all before

my friend's suicide   his father got me

that railway job helped   me survive abandonment

watch dead   winter trees torn

from a good friday train   ice storm damage

repaired most slowly   think of my friend

and death standing   water reflecting

trees upside down   a wild turkey observing

me train   and night ahead

never emerging   forever foraging

i come   to you by train
i leave you   by train most often
though sometimes   we leave together
but watch one   or the other of us
step off the train   to transfer you last night
waiting as i left   on a train i knew
i could wait too   for a later train but
instead went with   the others on the early
train you told me   later my next train
came just before or   just after your train
i text i'm here   when obviously here
can be anywhere   and often is
moving from place   to place across
the system train   by train and then
the movement at MacArthur   down steps and on
up the other side   one direction doing
that for the Richmond   train and the other
to get the Pittsburg/   Bay Point train criss-crossing
recrossing underneath   i'm motivated by multiple
desires those living   amongst trains all craving
steel rail screech   so i think we should
leave together tonight

3 TO 11 SHIFT TH&B RAILWAY, 1977

Critchley ran out of the caboose in Welland, psychotic break or high on something, buck-naked. Ran right down the tracks. The boys weren't sure what to do, No Toes Richards called it in to the dispatcher who was used to dealing with drunks on the road. Back here in Aberdeen yard Steve the radio operator had gone out to hit a bucket of golf balls from our parking lot back onto the golf course across the road. The guys from the Starlite had collected them from the back end of the railyard while waiting to head back to Toronto. We busted a gut imagining someone finding thirty golf balls sitting there. Dirty Bill had some hash oil, dipped his cigarette in it & asked me if I wanted a toke. Never done that before & did it mess with me, I was feeling pretty good. The midnight freight to Brantford was leaving same time as I was, they offered a ride on the train, let me hop off at the tracks by the apartment, never done that either, night of firsts & high besides, might have been a bad idea. They slowed down a bit for me to step off the engine. Wondering if my bad knee would hold. It did.

POEM FOR VANCOUVER

        9 cormorants skim English Bay's surface, in
a line stretching. 9 ocean-going freighters parked a mile out, wait
to be summoned past First Narrows to off-load cargo, spread across
English Bay's mouth, weight not just in holds, but in tonnes of carbon
to get here. That harbour seal spinning in the water, then under and
gone. Captain Vancouver landed in 1792, not first, that was José María
Narváez a year before. Back before any Europeans: so good later it had
to be clear-cut.
        Sitting on a bench by the Stanley Park Teahouse,
beside a broken clam left by a crow. Its flesh iridescent, open to air. The
Salish met Vancouver's ship with gifts, trade was good they thought, later
came the guns. Crow in the tree above has a problem. Shits on the next
bench, proclaiming his territory. Everything is about sex my therapist told
me, even not-sex is.

stone men, inukshuk,
stare out at a flat ocean
later they will drown
and then not drown and so on
nine cormorants surfacing

THIS IS A TRIBUTE FOR A MAN WHO IS NOT ALREADY DEAD

like a crow who picks
black bits into bits   hops over
what he leaves behind   others get
he is only forgiving himself or that rain seasons
a place beneath always
                              and then his reading
of gravel   death not feared or so said
his poetry   a choice made to stay
an understanding
of a deep well in his yard
where nothing bothers to remain
hidden
               tribute his
wife said is a sign of dependence
which gave her pause   this man
she has known and not
for many years   an instant   maybe a day

PHOTO #7

you asked me for a poet's
words and i gave

you these – *one wild and precious*
what will you

do with them or any
words given is really

indeterminate insubstantial
insouciant

meaning only
in context of a whole

life not a specific moment
in time like this photo

great whale
ribs on white

sand a grad-
uation of sorts

mountains at
sea a plaster cast

the portal to what
the future or the past

circling like the whale
who contained the ribs

in the imagination
before the country left

the country let's be
honest who wants

to be the one stepping
through a portal

ROCKY MOUNTAIN TALE

Pinus contorta, across the river
their green tips laden with cones,
cliff face spotted orange with
Xanthoria elegans! A woman and
two non-specific dogs walking
on blue-white ice. My coffee
getting cold.

As again in my mind Greg ties
the knot around his neck, in his fifties
forgotten by most. In Argentina
Colgate toothpaste is a hard sell,
colgáte: hang yourself.

It's different for landscape,
river cuts a new channel.
The old one fills with dirt, a scar
of how it was before,
not any better or worse
you might say, just takes more
time than we have.

Last night my co-worker got
me drunk and stoned, said she
wanted me to lose my inhibitions.
Takes a lot for that to happen,
guess I won't do anything

about it, wait for the universe. Which doesn't
seem to know how to knock on my door,
apparently waits outside in bushes
rather than approach like someone normal.
Though normal continues to devour
its own from what I've seen.

DEMENTIA

they were
all younger it is

                      a memory

that comes

                      back perhaps

not even a
memory now

                      more a

rough

                      of what was who

then who
he thinks he remembers

                      how he

thinks

boys drowned in
white churn
below
cataracts they
all swam there but
boys
drowned
    his faith –

not here, but
yesteryear

                            thinks

            he drove out
to the lake house they thought
              him crazy   there and back
              same day
wanted her
              to want him   a '55 Pontiac
              Star Chief   fins he wants   chrome lots of chrome

UNTITLED

I mean like on this planet at this time
I mean like driving over high bridges and wondering if you'll make it
I mean like not expecting your combination lock to work though it always
    does but yet still not expecting it
I mean like watching your friend doing drunk yoga on a back patio at 2 a.m.
I mean like those dreams where you are driving from the back seat and it
    never seems to go well
I mean like watching that raven in the tree singing and both you and the
    raven know it is ridiculous but likely portentous
I mean like Patty Wilson necking with you in the gym at your high
    school dance and you not realizing it was because she like liked you and
    how you won't realize it until forty years later and only then because it
    is explained to you
I mean like being hemmed in on the 401 at that section where there are
    sixteen lanes and you feel like your arms are growing longer and longer
I mean like after a nightmare you wake up and go into the bathroom
    and something horrible is in the mirror and turns out you are still in a
    nightmare but it's way worse and your unconscious has done that to you
I mean like screaming at God at the bottom of the stairs
I mean like those four ravens hanging out all the time near where you sit
    and how they never seem to be too worried about risks or explanations

LISTEN, SELF, I HAVE SOME THINGS YOU NEED TO KNOW –

Sit up straight vessel   find five crows chased by
twelve gulls   their uncreased wheeling
morning   meet a man named
Ray   he lives
everywhere   says he always buys the jumbo-sized
cherries   you won't regret your latest
decision   at least not
immediately   that brings
us to now   the weasels have
fallen   their inherent slipperiness almost saving you –
                as you counter your core beliefs surfacing rising
                     cream grey tide on up
                         unconsciously blue voices in
             pecked black –
                low tide will express geese and rocks all as one in
the slumbering light   recall bits of nothing   bits of geese and rocks
bits of long-legged bird among secreted Second Beach bathers
                         his face staring before him
                          seaweed-encrusted stone
                            reflected sky
two small children   a boy and a girl   stand in for the blue woman

WHILE DRINKING GRANVILLE ISLAND LAGER @YYC FEBRUARY 12TH 4 P.M.

warm wind

  sweetened through mountain
passes grizzlies asleep
in soft caves
     dream dreams of blood
on railway tracks
            haints
  whistle in the valley
a warning a call
to living
on the dead years
of death to feed on the builders
are here too tearing up ground digging
toward the centre ripping down
the old notice

air something wrong
    happy

    mountains

  foretell an end

     today's sky blue cloud
  shifting above chinook
winds know

ON LEAVING

the dog down the
street that has
been driving you
crazy with

its barking when
you go to bed is
missing it is fall that
time of

murmurations
but no the starlings
don't seem to

be around this
year the
squirrels and
chipmunks have

abandoned your
yard robots
are not
calling

your cellphone
to tell you

about a free

cruise you've won
again Facebook stops

suggesting young

women in
bikinis in

New Zealand

as friends even

though you
have no friends

in common you
are staring

at your door

MARRIAGE

early on you
and i'd spend
sunday afternoons
watching the living-
room furniture
move one way
then the next
sometimes the couch
ended up on the back
wall sometimes blocking
the kitchen door
sometimes way over under
the window on the front
wall occasionally on
the ceiling the rest
of the stuff
wherever it chose
it would never be
perfect it'd run
out of time or
patience or both
"good enough for now"
we'd say but it'd be
back at it a week
or two later
alone i watched crows
and squirrels last
night arrange
themselves the crows
funeral dancing in
their way
the squirrels busy
ignoring
me they live in
the deep business

of leaping
that couch
shifted across the room
trying to find
a place until
it was finally
wholly comfortable
in its own
defeat but by
then i'd moved
to the opposite coast

MIDNIGHT COASTAL

stars wend towards basement   you know your parents

dwell on your return feigning sleep   while the poor creak

outside windows you vomit   ambrosia the full moon

wander your path darkly   there is no path

no moon not something   to build a life the sand shifts

beneath collapsing you   clothes hung out

to dry is a dead pelican   lost in duplicity

beaches waiting with   no faith all mole crab

digging out and digging back in   night leaves you

wanting more desire a thing   you think when you finally rise

day has abandoned not   you but the rest

ON THE ROAD: BLUE WATER BRIDGE (THE BORDER)

Above you –
sky surrenders itself against horizon
and far below – the St. Clair River,

      unrelentingly blue as well,

drains the Upper Great Lakes, 2.5 billion
gallons per day. The two great countries'
border suffocated by transport
trucks and security like the air has
been let out of all the tires.

      No one disputes it.

On both sides the dance
marathon of the industrial heartland slowly
winds down, no one the wiser or happier.

In Canada the West is burning and bunged up
on oil, the East is measuring itself
with humidex, but trees
look to lengthening nights,
begin to consider colouring and
dropping their leaves.
      Almost time, almost.

And at this precise second –

a small white Fiat on
the Blue Water Bridge drives
away from the swaying
and (for better or for worse)
onto the solid ground of America.

NATURAL HISTORY

my friend says imagine this
think of mountain peaks

as sky islands and
below a hostile matrix
i say i'd rather think

you're a hostile matrix
he says fuck you

and we continue on in silence
walking down a road

definitely having taken a wrong turn
my friend says imagine this

you're a hostile matrix
or are you a mountain peak
a guy in a yard yells at us

i don't know where you've come from
but it's the fastest way out of here

we don't know what that means
but it makes all the difference

fuck you we both say to him
and continue on

AT A SLOUGH IN EUGENE

       sara and i stand
above amazon creek's
oil-slow waters
early evening shadows side
by each companions motioning
reflected voices all blurred blood
rushing towards blood silence
and erasure i understand
               nothing –

memories longing
purposelessness
          there once was
a woman
cliff-edge at bow falls
wondering how i got
there rapids far below a story
i hadn't ever heard i didn't
enjoy heights her sure-footedness
convinced me a magpie
once walked through her
body and saved her

      my foot slipped as twilight
entered my body i accept
safety as desire only
when there is nothing left
and everything
is in relationship to failing
             each day

brings its own light which cannot
be owned she may have felt
that way too but in that it is
all like yesterday cold stone

unclimbed mountains
where language fails completely

blueness all up under this chanting –

ON A BEACH

You would call this too clichéd for a poem, a couple on a January beach in
Northern California holding hands as large waves break in front of them,
a roar that doesn't stop, heard first from beyond the berm of sand, in the
parking lot but now encompassing their small world of plovers and walk-
racing sanderlings. Tiny birds confronting the infinite.
                         Yes, even with the couple's black dog sniffing
yesterday's detritus, seafoam washing in, wind tearing off small pieces
and dispersing them across sand. Maybe the man is thinking about the
scene from *From Here to Eternity* (though far too cold today for that but he
can't help it) as the waves do their thing, maybe the woman is rubbing his
hand, some warmth for chilled fingers. (I'm not sure what she is thinking
but I'm pretty sure they are deeper thoughts than his.) The sky is blue
though,

deafeningly so, and you of course
would call that clichéd, as a sanderling
avoids the clamouring
surf. You with all your rules.

ALBA FOR CONTRA COSTA

Here overhead a pair of overly
iconic golden eagles achieve
a best-ever year or more often one
under-appreciated vulture positions
us well patience awaiting opportunity

Here light reverses in evening in
whatever environment we operate slowly
erasing burnished hilltops highlights
benefits associated with integration below –
the deep rooted have survived summer again

and here ravens and fox squirrels focus
on what we can't control from roof
to ground to tree to roof again
a delivery on commitments
never silent among oak leaf litter

A WALK BY LAKE MERRITT

She says it's more about what we are called by,
some confusion about politics themselves,
how mothers sometimes think the opposite or go by feelings,
she's given up telling people what to do.
It's one thing to feel sad it's another to talk non-stop about it, she says.
Something I need to keep in mind, I think.
I say, like the Stones said,
she says, I think I know the song but not that lyric.
She hates bare hills, they make her feel claustrophobic.

Above Oakland a supermoon, which the internet says won't occur again
for almost twenty years but we both remember the internet saying a
similar thing a few months ago and rain is coming not long from now we
can tell.

We stop. Look at the moon.
She's thinking about when she'll see it again like that.
I'm thinking I'll be dead.

THE HANGING MAN

In a day of deep meditation, others saw him, sensed his presence. They were he and he welcomed them. I did not, he did not. Instead of Jungian archetypes I fell asleep and dreamed of SUV headlights and a pond with bulrushes. That's okay, Brother Camillus said, we're all different, it isn't a competition. But of course it was.

The others crying over their insights and heartfelt experiences where I mostly caught up on my sleep. How about enlightenment, I thought. I'm ready, bring it on. The Buddha said, I am awake, I had to say I was asleep. It was about then the hanged man showed up, his head buried in brown dirt, his foot

tied to a crossbeam. Hey, I said, you shouldn't do that, but he said he had no choice. That was his fate. You can make yourself feel better by turning him upside down and saying he's dancing a jig. But it is a reminder of the jig other hanged men do, you know, like my friend Greg.

How Greg has only shown up in dreams, airport arrivals glowing gold, and how does that make sense. He said he was okay, seemed more than okay but dead of course. I know that. Death being the next archetype to be studied in this floating ground, breathing deep to fall deep.

CORMORANTS DIVING

exciting at first / then sad / watching the cormorant-fishing ~ Bashō

i am a two-
year-old learning i debated

all afternoon were those
birds floating out in far
water and diving – loons
or cormorants? in the end
the answer appears

~

Bashō would have remained
excited on this day no need
for later sadness today is
a student in a swimming
pool's deep end on the surface –

legs and arms kick / twelve feet above the bottom / the air a cloud
enveloping

~

rocks lined on the edge
teak chairs
aging in place asking
"What is that bird?"
"Song Sparrow
Ross" and again

breaking laps my feet / calling out the birds / "Egret" "Osprey" "Same
Osprey"

~

O Bashō, what else can i say?

she was beautiful / and was once loved / how alone in the dark

~

there are days i have had the whale-bone ring around my neck the leash
holding me i was born to do it hauled back to the boat and the fish dug
out of my throat it is like that some days first exciting then sad

POEM FOR THE TREE SQUIRRELS OF CALIFORNIA

There are those who write about the legal status of eastern fox squirrels in California (an invasive squirrel), allowable ways to kill them (pretty well anything), how they can be detected (apparently you just watch for them). I want to say those people are seriously misguided. Eastern fox squirrels do not exhibit sexual dimorphism but the bad luck of the eastern fox squirrel is he is from away, native grey squirrels are protected and a licence issued by the State of California is needed to kill one of the grey ones but nothing is required to kill our friend eastern fox squirrel. Does eastern fox squirrel understand this? How precarious his life is compared to his grey brethren? An eastern fox squirrel the other day was planking cutely in the quad, Kayla taking his picture with her iPhone. She could have been instead dispatching him with a hammer as allowed under California State Law. It hardly seems fair the value placed on being from here.

Dark January days, rain soaking him like a hundred-dollar bill.

POEM FOR THE SEWER CATS OF ST. MARY'S

Your life is not that of tiny deer or wild turkeys,

Heads poke out of sewer pipes, slouch through

Culverts and hedges, pad beneath and through

Ancient (or at least oldish) walls.

What is it that brings you here?

The brothers who inhabit these places know

That value of living outside hard human order,

That devotion of small things to small places,

Leaving wideness for tight freedom.

What special talent do you bring to this world?

12 DANCERS ON 12 TABLES

Otherwise we are lost ~ Pina Bausch

spread across the quad
                           dramatists, tables
don't think
      about what tables mean
just get on
      tables and do the thing
dancers slow spin on tables

we here go, they say
one at a time
before silence shifts
under blue sky take it all
in examine closely all details . . .
"here" "we" "go"

crow above faster crow adds his input whole other duet thing

really beautiful

partially about quality
                           in bodies cultivate sensation anger
                     floating take ownership right away

okay think we're done

beneath white pillars
some of you   drop
some of you   praying beneath
ready   go again

cue you every night girl open-mouth at crow
flies over hops over broken ways walks over old man arthritic knees way
long boards to bookstore

that's a mess but looks really nice
ending in applause

BOLTED LANDSCAPE

standing at the crossroads a place called vista:
I 680's George Miller Jr. Memorial Bridge (southbound)
Congressman George Miller Bridge (northbound)
across Carquinez Strait   oil refineries
either end   Shell Martinez   Tesoro Martinez

Valero (née Exxon) Benicia   rusted
stretch of railroad bridge   Union Pacific Railroad
Benicia-Martinez Drawbridge (1928)
up the middle
a red-tailed hawk (*Buteo jamaicensis*) conservation status:

"of least concern, population increasing"
curve of concrete I 680 overpass behind
and above me
simple: mountain
sky   water   hawk

WE WILL DRIVE

cross country,
lightning
late strobe
interior
of clouds
in dark
above
Motel 6
in Bloomington
pink ponytailed
old men
undershirts
motorcycle
buy live bait
from Missouri
vending machines
deluge
in Oklahoma City
"that's Oklahoma"
they tell us
giant dinosaur
hugs Route 66
sign Amarillo's
Big Texan
giant windmills
strewn across
the nation
blading with
the effort
it takes to save
the planet
left turn
at Albuquerque
corrected
Meteor City

a busted
trading post
sign to nowhere
Mother Road
takes us
a flow of traffic
that is never
dust devils usher
the way across
Mojave
so we can see
an awful movie
and finally eat
salad at Mega Burger

all those bluebirds

LAC-MÉGANTIC

Observe – slim moon, usual July stars,
clean night breeze. They've put railway tracks right down the middle of
this small-town street, as if inviting the multitude to descend.

        A bar in the centre of town called Musi-Café. A band takes a
break around then, a guitarist   outside smoking. A
couple at a table on the patio. They are fortyish and met here tonight
by   accident. A friend leaves at 1 a.m. for her car,
winks at them.

Rotting
fruit smell of oil.
        What
emerges from feeding our addiction –
20 million pounds of steel and Bakken crude oil on fire,
47 people killed, 5 of them vaporized.

        The local hospital said
no injuries got treated, they were all dead already.
The young firefighter pulled his ex-
girlfriend from wreckage, committed
suicide three and a half months later.

receive back your names   enumerate your ages
you   how you left Musi-Café   left your friend   your brothers   how
you were singing you   tell us how you prayed every matin at 4 a.m.
your bénédictions asked for   received you   your little sister slept under
the sky's black curve   your souls to keep   stars once reflecting   waters
once unoiled   Lake of Place-Where-the-Fishes-Are-Held

LAS VEGAS TAXI RIDE

On the way here the driver explained
the world. Said it's lawyers,
hookers and cab drivers

who know it all, carry everyone's stories.
A woman told him she was married to a good man,
good since he didn't beat her.

Told him a story where she said luckily
she had been raped before so she knew
what to do.

Where he came from (a country that no longer exists)
you just expected to be stopped
at any time.
        How if you complained they took you
somewhere quiet and then you didn't complain
anymore ever.
        His iPad now tracks his speed, reports
his exceedances instantly back to the dispatcher.
He's comfortable with that.

That girl in the Vegas hotel lobby dressed
as a raccoon is the normal one. She knows
she belongs here, her fake skin comfortable.

I watched the front yards
dying along the road as he talked.

WHAT I WOULD SAY THEN

There's a huge Exxon refinery in Torrance, CA
The ESP on its catalytic cracker's ass
Exploded this summer, the plant came down hard
Grumbling Californians had to pay more for their gas

The electrostatic precipitator on that cat's ass
Turns out hard to repair, Exxon won't even talk to the EPA
Californians say they pay too much for their gas
Be down 'til at least next year so they now say

Hard to fix, they won't even talk to our EPA
Exxon's selling it to PBF, who told them to fix it first
Be down 'til at least next year, they reluctantly say
The place runs on California tar, no kidding the worst

They're selling it to PBF, but it's Exxon's to fix first
There's nowhere else for that crude to go
The place runs on California tar, really the worst
It makes lots of petcoke, not so good as you know

There's nowhere else for dirty crude to go
Hey, then why not leave it in the ground
Then petcoke doesn't get made, so
You could wrap that place in a shroud

Hey, why not leave it in the ground
Imagine we all got together, shut in the oil
And they could wrap that place in a shroud
Our warming planet would thank us all

Imagine: we all get together, shut in the oil,
The plant stays down forever plus a day
There was once a refinery in Torrance, CA

POEM FOR ME

Rise above your sweet sad self, an entire audience
        watches. We say we are not just granite made

grateful, but then whoever matches bluster with
        solemnity. Our future is not our poem, our birthright

bought and paid for. Though we are not entirely
        compliant, we seek the poet's arc and only ask

for what we are willing to lose. At once we are both
        rent and worn, time has proven itself futile.

We understand that better than most. You and your
        imperfect reflexive past, you and the dogs

of your missing, you and your thoughts' cardboard
        crayon scrawl: What is ever finally found?

Sprint, Day-Glo Buddha instructs. Fly
        higher, the dream nods. Your imaginary

future a frantic gasping – everything
        else irreducible truths. Your eyes, for example,

erased blackboards you continue to ignore. Yesterday
        was all chainsaw, today is all chicken. Tomorrow

jackhammer or sheep, who's to say? Like the crow standing
        smack dab in the middle of the road or the deer fly

burrowing into your hair seeking suicide – all exactly as
        your plain sad way.

TODAY WE MOVE TO
CLIMATE CHANGE HOURS

we left town for the cabin, deserved
the break from full-on working,
full-on drinkable lives, fumes
collecting and rising on their own
specified terms, Nickelback on
the radio and IHateMimes.com
on the iPad, yearning for the old
knocking engine, what we used to call
ping, the car drove the Sierras, NPR

told us of COP21 in Paris fixing
the line on climate change morph, bored
pols to sing off the crowds, while we sang
off our hearts only we had tire chains
and change for the jukebox, damage
was done, or would be at the appropriate
time as agreed to by all the parties per
memorandum of understanding
assignable but non-binding, beyond

the car door an off-ramp,
cars filling a void, fully awed us
requiring attention to literary,
to emotional, to frequently held space,
long slow turn, the steep
grade check your brakes first,
they say running out of road
the problem we have never reality
from our political friends smiling away

BEFORE RED FLAG AND BURNING

today's pale bled sky says i am old
all these numbered
        friends left

of yellowing equations
left behind bereft wizened

        alcohol this
parable-self nominated recursing
if not resurrecting abandonment

moon an evacuated day land-shaped
        destitute shore

dog walker her tribes
12 meanwhile hidden crayfish
begin conjuring meanwhile

these truths tired
        afraid half-life

barrens broken perhaps
        all true
the instant this instance ahead

        November rains straightened
defined by intersections bounded

erasures and deft silences
a choice or not every
        fork curved

hand slipping thickened fingers
quicksilver cunning worn wooden

worm-eaten table set for 12 plus 1
        body stretched
on piled bones beach-caved

ribs loosed brown-grey long necking hook
        on beak

the sardine population
        collapsing waves
ripped open those Diablo winds

good come she says
        treat in her hand

SOMEONE

              _ died early
      , still dead, wash
My hands now

White church lit at night
Heavy wooden doors tightly shut

Where do I go, it's
           Difficult choices, a
Strawberry moon

You are not there often

I am always here

The metal gate bangs shut
    The door locked solid behind
          Me, you suffered and never said

Both thinking we should end
It, neither will when allowed

Small blacktail tries
    To decide, make a move
        Locked in position

Here not important   There not important

I've often wondered about
Driving across the continent
Finish a singular objective

You try all your
          Life, I try to be good

There are effective ways

She said I put you on a pedestal

Feet of Gucci she said

The truth not wanted
I'd know all the lies
                    Wander late night streets at
                    4 a.m., when the world is real
                    Empty, most hollow wind
Not a very good time
That's not what you mean

          There is a strong odour
          It can't be ignored this
Time, and yet here we are

Once it made sense
Living in hope I asked

          How dead is it precisely
          It hasn't moved for a decade
Not near dead enough

A life to serve
Coffee, no cream, no sugar

Snow never
Falls here, roads
Steep, traction still an issue

Slipping by, time

And some materials

A balcony never finished
        A road never started
The river at night, babbles

I ran as hard as I could
Black canvas PF Flyers

This is neither this nor that
        The crow from chair to ground
She really doesn't care

You said it was
Time, I say no

                        An old man sits outside

Warming in the empty yard
The sun never refuses

Once the dog ran from us
Never to be looked for

                        Vultures have left, thermals
                            Rise without them, sky
                                Darkens early now

You are always up early
Night too much for you

                        Caffeine drives me

hard
Heart's fast beat, hands
Shaking, yet it feels so good

Time for a lot of thinking   And time to decide nothing

In this place snow does fall

                              Cliff edge blocked by drifts
                              Sleet pits a face

All I have done to this point
Pretty sure I know very little

                    How light shines at dusk
              Hills pink and gold, all
        Swaddled in darkness

Platitudes are well and
Good, until I get hurt

Crippled things outside
Wandering night's highway
A light on in the house ahead

Crow again, on the ground
The chair, in the tree

PHOTO #10

mountains explain everything and are here once again
their railway scars
       receding for a change
as you walk loudness outrage and fens

here is where the elk took the wolf pack
here is where you found Jesus
okay not Jesus at least
       climate change

this is where tracks cross
       the valley floor built
to last they thought for a while
lay carbon on our hands

and subtler forms of dying
walk faster you tell yourself you won't notice
and eventually
       you catches up with you

glaciers recede and snowpacks shorten in your
lifetime a life in your life
       a shortening
of breath of heaviness lack of lackness

it adds up it seems to not much
but then mountains
have always talked
       to mountains the conversation when

you go to bed when you dream when
you wake they close in on you today
       this place is known and
avoided by its native people

J

Rain dropping
like responsibilities
and it
may or may
not solve things,
like California
drought or your
own lack of
interest, a
Pineapple
Express
straight from
the Philippines,
here it is and
keeps coming
as you both walk
soaking along
Powell to
Biscuits and
Blues. J has
lived here
her whole
life and
never gone,
the woman at the front jokes J should tip big then since the club's been
here twenty-one years, the woman's friend giggling, slapping her arm.
                    Twenty-one years ago, X clinically depressed,
it was all over between you and Y. Over a beer: categorized, put away
so you didn't worry, J says, you put your anger in a bucket and with that
understanding you made the world an experiment –

you remember how Y was easy to get over, how you found that equation of small annoyances, her airily attending that Irish Republican Army fundraiser for one –

Results and Conclusions: "When checking with female acquaintance the act of checking seems to agitate female subject creating a new state. A feelings check not always right approach to relationship dynamics. Many false readings. Confirmed with alternate subjects."

– lack of emotional authenticity, J says, comes at a price.

CAT CATCHER

If you and every person on the planet caught
all the cats and put them in a big box we would know
so much more than we do now. I think I would
take Schrödinger's bet – the cat's alive.
No, it's dead. Oh, I don't know. Cats don't like being
put in a box at all. 600 million cats
on the planet and a good number of them are wild.
But I'm not going to talk about "The Naming of Cats"
or musicals. You can thank me later. Cats,
which are to say felines, are only mentioned
in the bible once and that is in the deuterocanonical
Book of Baruch, meaning it helps to be Catholic to get
the reference. A mystery that continues to this day.
Surprisingly, some cats are unholy and full of natural sin.
I am entertained by the common name of the wind.
At least when first heard. My own cat's
Doppelgänger sits outside the window
right now. And once heautoscopically was on the other end when
I traversed the continent. When my white cat's vardøger
wanders the world occasionally his long claws trap him
on long carpet fibres, tapered curved needles
in ancient tapestries. Think back. What if eight-year-old
you were riding your green CCM home from school,
through a new subdivision after a heavy rain,
and you abandoned your stuck bike in mud. How perfect
would you be then. I can tell you. Your mother and father
never fought, a tourniquet applied, the bleeding
staunched before it started. The cat
left outside, crying, after the break-in.
My father up early every day, a cigarette
butt floating in the toilet. Sometimes,
mid-lick, a cat will hork a tight
elongated cylinder of hair. I think you know
exactly what I mean. It takes a lot of gacking. Not on the floor –
that would be too convenient – but on laundry

or pillow or somewhere I'll step on it.
Sometime not too distantly – that would be too convenient –
I'll blow up my life like I'm blowing up this
poem and I will wonder whether it was the right
thing to do. Just before all that, my life
will sit on its haunches, staring unblinking,
licking a paw with her tiny
pink diamond tongue.

LANDSCAPES OF THE SMALL HOURS

We walk lines in dark,
Lake Ontario's irregular
beat over us, moon
yet or not

yet full above the city. Pipelines or rail
                    lines, no matter, rusted
hum under
everything we do, a panic
        drive, the beat-up Ford Fairlane
        from Aberdeen to Fisher
yards, beat locomotives hauling
        steel coil, farm implements, flour,

        fertilizer. No matter,
the city
        sleeps while we travel
        and veer on loose railed ballast and creosote.
The
Downstairs John,
Phoenix,
Rathskeller,
Paddy Greene's,
Corktown,
Rose and Thistle,
Hanarhan's –

we quaff in them all
precisely
like
April snow
coarse granular damp disappearing.

THE ONE QUESTION I SHOULD BE ASKING

Why didn't I stop to clear ice
from the wipers? Or why didn't I
buy winter tires or new tires
or stay home?

Why look towards
oncoming traffic instead of away like I'd
been warned –
                    that slide on a white
ice corner, the inevitable coming together
and inevitable coming apart.

                    My life that went on, driving
that same highway every day,
rounding that same corner
with something like gratitude.

Why didn't I care? The one question.

TUNDRA SWANS

It's the way their necks twist
backwards
          over their bodies,
                              interleaved
feathers
          adrift on black water,

makes me wonder about myself,
about a complicated life.

The birds crowding
          early March open water
in front of me,
a ten thousand mile journey of ten thousand swans
broken here.

The tail feathers burn white fire
in mid-afternoon sun,
          wind whispering among whistling wings.

          What have they seen from above
with their jet-black eyes?
Open beaks judge,
the groans, the squawks scold.
          Dark webbed feet flurry over water.
                              The white wild air,

the final lift, ascension.

I know spring will come
but tonight
          pale green wrought iron chairs
          sit covered in snow at the edge
echoed in glass city.

THIS DARK

I don't know much beyond
what I've always known –

white cat asleep beside me,
a small silver Buddha on my desk in late evening

and sometimes my head bent
in quiet prayer on a grey afternoon.

Listen, my love –
      for that is what I need most –

in my dream you beside me. Wind
batters blinds above the bed, the window wide.

And when I wake and reach
      for you, the sheets cold.

Or is it the other way around?
You here beside me and the dream
an empty bed.

CHINOOK

need dwells   reciprocally I'm afraid
– you have trouble too
(push/on)   a short film running backwards (flickering)
      past my stop
          asleep
  on the bus
awake
  all night staring

I am mercury
next to it
     (rabbits)
malleability
   is what
     I want instead
more stress-damage

desire versus arousal
     woke to uninhabitable truth/non-truth
     (There are coyotes outside)
arousal vs. desire

to be honest it is very hard
to be honest you are very hard
to be honest I don't want to at all

AND LAKE ENDS / HERE
UNDER THE SKYWAY BRIDGE /

silver tailings / post-industrial ooze /
wire strung from steel towers / anchored
to another world / from historic gales /
where typhoid ships sat waiting
for the dying to get it over with / large
black dogs pile over sand / waves own
the thin shore / here is where you always walk /
what brings you into this time-lapsed night? /
wailing wind near empty beach /
grayling gulls' screamings drowned by this
sledge of dark surf / uncomfortable
observer / drinking and smoking at the corner
bar in humid August night air / clothes sticking / a woman
waits / back again to her work / the dead back
again too / the dead sitting beside you
hissing distrustful secrets / half remembered
truths / wrong memories of the wrong person /
the dead make quick work of your pride / quick work
of arrogance / 4:00 a.m. awakening / moon
sliding out / whispers in a deer soft night /
closet door ajar / it worries you / a late night walk over
the bridge / a man holding on having changed
his mind / police moving slowly towards him /
arms wrapped around steel pipe above
the abyss /

QUESTIONS SHOULD BE ASKED

There are words I keep forgetting
like *possum* or *spoon*. Sometimes I feel
them behind other words. There are dark
shadows under my eyes.

What are those birds?
What is this wilderness?
(my eyes are closed
on the 100D Flemingdon Park bus)

When I was small I came to this city, pigeons strutted the sidewalk
and short, old Italian men pushed red carts by the museum, roasting
chestnuts. My mother bought a small white bag for me. It was warm in
my palm, a burnt aroma as I peeled brown skin from hot meat. All the dry
leaves blew down the avenue and away into the fall sun.

(open my eyes)

       A man depends on
       A memory of his father and mother
       Or last lover
       A small white bag in an open palm
       And then he can go into the world
       Where he will learn about winning and failure
       One day he is playing with his best friend
       In the playground
       And next thing
       They are sitting on a park bench
       Looking at the scar that runs down his old-man chest

(this is my stop)

A man busking at Bloor and Avenue Rd.
tells me angels will dance in the sky the night he dies,

a white pigeon pumpjacks his head,
I cannot be sure of anything,

maybe shadows at dusk,
every day I am filled and then emptied, I can only

hope it begins again.
A man depends on

a memory of his mother or father
or a small white bag in an open palm.

(this is one of five places I sleep at night)

What I have done, what I have
failed to do, in my thoughts
and in my words.

I woke up one day and realized half of what is me
had left while I slept.

BLACK AND WHITE IMAGE OF FROZEN BEACH: LAKE ERIE ICE STRETCHED OUT TO OPEN WATER'S THIN BLADE, SUN HIGH, REFLECTION OF SUN A SHINING PATH ACROSS A WATER HORIZON, ACROSS BUCKLED ICE, ACROSS SAND BLENDED WITH HARD SNOW BLENDED WITH SAND

I think she died that day
or maybe not until the next.
On the way to the hospital
I stopped and took the photo,
the ice, the water, sky – in real life not black and white but all Prussian blue
and set with an overly brilliant sun. I'm not saying it felt like death
exactly, more like the moment before
or the moment after and I remember thinking of a sparrow's song –
rapid and thin. There was no sparrow.
Beach and sky devoid of life except for the occasional explosive cracks of ice
as it shoved itself ashore.

O'HARE, TERMINAL TWO, CONCOURSE E, GATE E1

On my iPod Springsteen
sings about a long walk
home and I think of you,
transfusions, headaches,
in the end you said
you understood God.

The snow's trapped me here for hours.
Like on your last day, alone
in my car on the 403 at midnight,
sleet driven into my windshield,
snow sheets across the wide road.
I felt you, a shiver departing.

The de-icer shines lime,
a smear on wet tarmac. The jet,
    a giant praying mantis,
huddles against the glass, afraid to fly.
And that voice over and over.
Orange alert level.

My scuffed black shoes in the grey bin,
slowly receding.

REFLECTIONS AT FIFTY-SEVEN

Eleventh floor rented
      condo looking over
            Bloor Street West
white cat reflected beside me, 11:07 p.m.

A late night call,
      Michael said
            you hanged yourself,
no other way to tell me but to tell me.

After your memorial my friend Michael and I talked about you
in the Second Cup.
Not sure when things went so bad for him, maybe after
his father died, maybe after his divorce, maybe –

A rabbi behind us interrupted, You'll never know why.

Thirty years after high school, you weren't clear
what was going on, why you left the big job in Calgary,
what you did here, consulting you said but assistant
in a climbing gym it turned out.

You said – when you give up all toys, you miss them.

I see you all the time, remember
a cut glass of twelve-year-old Scotch, your note
to your housemate not to go downstairs,
an ingenious contraption of rope. So like you.

WHILE APPLE PICKING IV

cornering colouring, falling, falling,
falls
  and
  arthritic ache
   you will soon
have, crisp red
   into Fall:
an
earlier
  darkness, life
subject

to night more than day,

leaves colouring robins in

those same woods,
gathering, falls and brown leaf
despite day,

cornering robins
   in those
same woods, gathering
colouring colouring colouring
colouring robins

in
those same woods,
gathering
  colouring

robins in
those
same woods, gathering
cold,

the orchard,

cornering, falling,
falling, falling, falls

PHOTO #18

is full of police in black and white photos
we run streets with squad cars blazing

why a Starbucks you ask reasonably
they like to break

call our friends they are caged
if a man has a false leg

or is named nobody
then a freedom zone becomes strictly

speaking a place to lie down
armoured horses are polices' best

have to admit they seemed like people
and probably were at one point

thankful Whole Foods is open
and grateful for the wonder of it all

standing here outside the bar calling
if only we could leave for the coast

AFTER THE MOVIE

My friend Michael & I cross King Street West, dodging
traffic, arguing about the movie. He says he believes success
& happiness coincide – you can only have one if you have

the other. I say, No they don't have anything to do
with each other, that's like saying shoes are necessary
to own a coat. He says, But that *is* true,

no point having a coat to go outside if you don't
have shoes. There'll come a day you'll stay inside
for good if you don't have both.

I say, That sounds like you were happy before that day.
He says, You might have thought you were happy but
then you realized you were unsuccessful.

I say, What you mean by happiness sounds more like
a business arrangement. I say, Happiness isn't conditional.
He says, It's conditional on what it takes to be happy.

We're now standing in front of the Snooty Fox –
the old Westdale Theatre's marquee blinking half on
& mostly off across the street – & I hear my voice

saying what I say to myself all the time – Most
everyone's life is pretty well mediocre at best
& really should anyone ask for more?

Michael takes hold of my elbow. Yes, he says,
they can & fucking well should. Inside we order
Barking Squirrels from our bartender, burly & bearded.

The beer is dark, rich burnt orange. I sip it like
I have never seen beer before. Hey, I say, didn't
this conversation feel kind of like Marie Howe's

poem "After the Movie?" I was just thinking that,
says Michael. Though this sure isn't New York City
& you aren't nearly as smart as the speaker

in that poem. Funny, I say, I was just thinking
how you aren't nearly as smart as her Michael.
We both sip our beer some more.

What are you up to tomorrow? says Michael.
But what I think he is saying is –
You are a failure, you should stay in your house forever.

Then I think, Does he know I want to remain
bewildered? The noise level is rising, laughter
from somewhere, glasses clinking

somewhere. Although we just got to the bar
we both have been here a very long time.
I say, Try not to become a man of success said Einstein.

Michael says, Idleness is fatal only to the mediocre
said Camus. Our bartender jumps in, Stupidity
lies in wanting to draw conclusions said Flaubert.

The three of us are quiet, thinking about failure
& success & thinking about nothing
& thinking about what jerks the others are.

Outside the marquee blinks no-blinks,
red tail lights blur on King Street West,
down the side street I know

my perfectly squat house sits perfectly
darkly quiet, at the end of that street is the trail
into the woods where nocturnal beasts wander.

HAPPINESS

In the elevator with mirrors
on four sides that puts
on ten pounds and twenty
years, I'm grateful you said
I can choose to be happy.
Or sad, I stride out into
a shit-filled city armed with
my own shit-eating grin.
      A blond curl
on Sunday
mornings, light
behind the blinds,
lids fluttered then
opened and then began
our cornflower day.
      My mouth against
yours, the first pebble
dropped into a first pond.
      It's not that I thought
it would go on.
But you go off
and choose happy
while I stare at two or more
fucked-up choices,
the middle of our
story gone, its porch
light turned off.

ACKNOWLEDGEMENTS

I am very grateful to Noelle Allen for publishing this collection, Carmine Starnino for his wonderful suggestions and Ashley Hisson for taking such care.

I would like to single out Brenda Hillman for gratitude, who I met at the Community of Writers Poetry Workshop in 2015 and who invited me into a poetry and life-changing experience at Saint Mary's College of California. Brenda is the best. And to thank Matthew Zapruder for his generous sharing of his deep knowledge and passion for poetry. Matthew is also the best. As well as Geoffrey G. O'Brien for his great encouragement and openness. All three poets have had a major influence on this collection.

Also thanks to Chris Sindt, Arisa White and Juliana Spahr for their valuable insights as faculty at Saint Mary's. I am especially grateful to my cohort in poetry at Saint Mary's: Sara Burant who shared so much of that poetic adventure with me and has continued to, Dan Alter, Tamara Miller, the late Andrea Murphy, Kayla Scullion Farrer, Cameron Stuart and Katie Walker. And to all my other friends at Saint Mary's and the Bay Area that came from this experience, particularly the cohort ahead and after mine in poetry. Thanks to Marc Castonguay for driving out to California with me, don't think I'd have made it there otherwise.

Thanks to those mentors over the years at the Banff Centre for the Arts and Creativity, including Karen Solie, Hoa Nguyen, David O'Meara, Fred Stenson, Alison Pick, Robert Hilles, Anne Simpson and Liz Philips. And to all those writers and artists I've met there and the late night conversations and other adventures. And Jim and Chip Olver for the paddling and always warm welcome in Banff.

Thanks to the Community of Writers Poetry Workshop in California for the transformative experience. Thanks especially to the generous faculty Brenda, Robert Hass, Sharon Olds, Forrest Gander, Evie Shockley and J. Michael Martinez.

Thanks to the Key West Literary Seminar and Jane Hirshfield for letting me join at the last minute to Jane's workshop, which has been an influence on this collection and my thinking about poetry.

Thanks to my long-time Hamilton poetry workshop group where I learned so much: Dick Capling, Linda Frank and Marilyn Gear Pilling. And for the workshop in Don McKay's kitchen in St. John's.

And to Heather, Neil, Alison and Erinn for their loving support. And for Owen, Chloe and Carson for being themselves.

NOTES

POEM FOR VANCOUVER – The poetic form is a haibun. This poem was in the suite of poems "Nothing Bothers to Remain" long-listed for the 2018 CBC poetry prize.

THIS IS A TRIBUTE FOR A MAN WHO IS NOT ALREADY DEAD – A response to a panel at AWP16 in tribute to the poet Donald Revell.

PHOTO #7 – The Photo # poems were written using a procedural prompt for an ekphrastic response to the poet's own photos. A random number was generated to choose a photo from the ranked list of "most interesting" as selected by the photo site Flickr's algorithm for interestingness. The italics in Photo #7 are from Mary Oliver's poem "The Summer Day." The sculpture *217.5 Arc x 13* by Bernar Venet in the photo is on permanent display at Sunset Beach in Vancouver.

WHILE DRINKING GRANVILLE ISLAND LAGER @YYC FEBRUARY 12TH 4 PM – A version of this poem is in the suite of poems "The Edge of Everything," finalist for the 2016 CBC poetry prize.

ON LEAVING – In the suite of poems "The Edge of Everything," finalist for the 2016 CBC poetry prize.

NATURAL HISTORY – This poem is an extended gigan. The gigan form was invented by Ruth Ellen Kocher. This poem adds two additional lines to the form.

CORMORANTS DIVING – The Bashō epigraph is from a Robert Hass translation.

POEM FOR THE SEWER CATS OF ST. MARY'S – *St. Mary's* refers to Saint Mary's College of California and *brothers* refers to the De La Salle Christian Brothers who founded and still are involved in the operation of the university.

12 DANCERS ON 12 TABLES – In the suite of poems "The Edge of Everything," finalist for the 2016 CBC poetry prize.

BOLTED LANDSCAPE – In the suite of poems "The Edge of Everything," finalist for the 2016 CBC poetry prize.

LAC-MÉGANTIC – Forty-seven people were killed and half the small Quebec town destroyed in a crude train explosion at one a.m. in July 2013. This poem was in the suite of poems "Nothing Bothers To Remain," long-listed for the 2018 CBC poetry prize.

LAS VEGAS TAXI RIDE – Previously published in *Written Here: The Community of Writers Poetry Anthology, 2015*. Olympic Valley, CA: Community of Writers, 2015.

WHAT I WOULD SAY THEN – On February 18, 2015, there was an explosion at Exxon Mobil's Torrance, California, refinery that destroyed equipment and injured four people. Gasoline prices soared in California as the repairs took eighteen months. The form of the poem is a pantoum.

TODAY WE MOVE TO CLIMATE CHANGE HOURS – This poem was in the suite of poems "Nothing Bothers To Remain," long-listed for the 2018 CBC poetry prize.

PHOTO #10 – See Photo #7 above.

CAT CATCHER – This poem is in conversation with the Terrance Hayes poem "The Shepherd."

THIS DARK – Previously published in *Arc Poetry Magazine*, no. 68 (Summer 2012).

QUESTIONS SHOULD BE ASKED – Italics from the Roman Catholic Confiteor.

BLACK AND WHITE IMAGE OF FROZEN BEACH: LAKE ERIE ICE STRETCHED OUT TO OPEN WATER'S THIN BLADE, SUN HIGH, REFLECTION OF SUN A SHINING PATH ACROSS A WATER HORIZON, ACROSS BUCKLED ICE, ACROSS SAND BLENDED WITH HARD SNOW BLENDED WITH SAND – In the suite of poems "The Edge of Everything," finalist for the 2016 CBC poetry prize.

O'HARE, TERMINAL TWO, CONCOURSE E, GATE E1 – Previously published in *Arc Poetry Magazine*, no. 68 (Summer 2012); and Goyette, Sue. *The Best Canadian Poetry in English, 2013*. Toronto: Tightrope Books, 2013.

PHOTO #18 – See Photo #7 above.

AFTER THE MOVIE – This poem is in conversation with Marie Howe's poem "After the Movie."

Ross Belot is a poet, photographer, documentary filmmaker, and an energy and climate change columnist. He previously worked for a major Canadian petroleum company for decades before retiring in 2014. Now he writes ecopoetics and opinion pieces about government climate change inaction. Ross was a finalist for the CBC Poetry Prize in 2016 and longlisted in 2018. In 2017, he completed an MFA at Saint Mary's College of California. Born in Ottawa, Ross has made his home in the Golden Horseshoe since 1970.